AF480674

FEELING TO HEALING

THE ROLE OF EMOTIONAL INTELLIGENCE
IN CHILD DEVELOPMENT

DR. MINAKSHI BANSAL

Copyright © Dr. Minakshi Bansal
All Rights Reserved.

This book has been self-published with all reasonable efforts taken to make the material error-free by the author. No part of this book shall be used, reproduced in any manner whatsoever without written permission from the author, except in the case of brief quotations embodied in critical articles and reviews.

The Author of this book is solely responsible and liable for its content including but not limited to the views, representations, descriptions, statements, information, opinions and references ["Content"]. The Content of this book shall not constitute or be construed or deemed to reflect the opinion or expression of the Publisher or Editor. Neither the Publisher nor Editor endorse or approve the Content of this book or guarantee the reliability, accuracy or completeness of the Content published herein and do not make any representations or warranties of any kind, express or implied, including but not limited to the implied warranties of merchantability, fitness for a particular purpose. The Publisher and Editor shall not be liable whatsoever for any errors, omissions, whether such errors or omissions result from negligence, accident, or any other cause or claims for loss or damages of any kind, including without limitation, indirect or consequential loss or damage arising out of use, inability to use, or about the reliability, accuracy or sufficiency of the information contained in this book.

Made with ♥ on the Notion Press Platform
www.notionpress.com

Contents

Contents

Prayer

"Om Bhadram Karnebhih Shrinuyama Devah
Bhadram Pashyemakshabhiryajatrah
Sthirairangais Tushtuvamsastanubhih
Vyashema Devahitam Yadayuh
Svasti Na Indro Vriddhashravah
Svasti Nah Pusha Vishwavedah
Svasti Nastarkshyo Arishtanemih
Svasti No Brihaspatir Dadhatu
Om Shantih Shantih Shantih"

This mantra is a prayer for universal well-being, invoking the blessings of various deities for protection, health, and happiness. It emphasizes the importance of experiencing the auspicious through all senses and living a life aligned with divine purpose. The repetition of "Shantih" at the end signifies a deep desire for peace in the individual, the environment, and the universe at large. This mantra is often recited as a prayer for peace, prosperity, and the physical and spiritual well-being of all beings.

DEDICATION

This book is dedicated to all the parents, educators, and caregivers who devote their lives to nurturing the future. Your commitment to understanding and fostering emotional intelligence in children creates a brighter, more compassionate world. May this guide support you in your journey as you guide the next generation from feeling to healing.

ℬ

Dr. Minakshi Bansal, born in the bustling metropolis of Delhi, India, has led a life steeped in artistry, scholarly pursuit, and an unwavering commitment to societal betterment. Following her marriage, she relocated to Ahmedabad, Gujarat, where she has since blossomed into a multifaceted beacon of inspiration for many. Dr. Minakshi is not only recognized as a gifted artist in the realm of Fine Arts but also as an esteemed author, a devoted social worker and a dedicated research scholar in Psychology. Her journey, marked by a profound dedication to elevating those around her, especially the downtrodden and underprivileged children of society, is a testament to her deep-seated belief in the transformative power of engagement and empathy.

From her earliest days, Minakshi was distinguished by an insatiable appetite for reading. Her literary universe was inhabited by characters and narratives that spanned ethical tales, motivational and inspirational stories, and the mythic parables imbued with life lessons. This voracious reading habit was not merely for personal edification but was driven by a desire to distill and disseminate the essence of these narratives to foster the development of students and peers alike. She was particularly captivated by the lives and teachings of historical figures and spiritual leaders such as Adi Shankaracharya, Swami Vivekananda, Dr. APJ Abdul Kalam, Mahamana Pandit Madan Mohan Malviya, Mahatma Gandhi, Sardar Vallabhai Patel, and Vinoba Bhave, among others. Their philosophies and life stories fueled her ambition to embody their ideals of resilience, selflessness, and relentless pursuit of knowledge.

Dr. Minakshi's academic and practical engagement with psychology has been equally noteworthy. As a research scholar, her focus has been on exploring the intricate tapestry of the human psyche, aiming to unlock the potential for psychological well-being and societal harmony. Her scholarly work is complemented by her active involvement in social work, where she employs her academic insights to make tangible differences in the lives of the underprivileged. Her endeavours in social work are characterized by an innovative approach that combines traditional wisdom with contemporary psychological practices to address the multifaceted challenges faced by these communities.

Her artistic talents, another facet of her diverse capabilities, are not merely a personal passion but also serve as a medium through which she communicates and connects with others. Her art, rich in symbolism and emotional depth, reflects her philosophical inquiries and social concerns, offering viewers a glimpse into the breadth of her intellect and the depth of her compassion.

In addition to her contributions to the arts and social sciences, Dr. Minakshi has embraced the healing arts of Pranic Healing, mastering the techniques developed by Master Choa Kok Sui. This practice, which focuses on the manipulation of Prana or life energy to heal the body and aura, has been both a personal journey of discovery and a means through which she extends her healing touch to others. Her proficiency in Pranic Healing is complemented by her advocacy and teaching of various forms of meditation aimed at rejuvenation, personal betterment, and the cultivation of harmony within individuals and communities alike.

Dr. Minakshi's life is a narrative of relentless pursuit, not just of personal achievement but of the upliftment and empowerment of society at large. Her diverse interests and talents—spanning the arts, literature, psychology, and the healing practices—converge on a singular path of service. She embodies the spirit of the luminaries who inspired her, channelling their legacy through her actions and teachings. Through her books, art, and social initiatives, she continues to inspire a new generation to embark on their own journeys of self-discovery, resilience, and altruism.

Her commitment to social betterment, particularly her focus on uplifting underprivileged children, reflects a deep understanding of the transformative potential of education and personal development. By integrating her knowledge of psychology, her artistic sensibilities, and her healing practices, Dr. Bansal has developed a holistic approach to social work that addresses both the immediate needs and the long-term well-being of the communities she serves.

As an author, Dr. Minakshi's writings offer a blend of inspirational insights, practical wisdom, and reflective contemplations drawn from her extensive reading and life experiences. Her books serve as a guide for those seeking to navigate the complexities of life with grace, resilience, and purpose. Through her narratives, she extends an invitation to her readers to explore the depths of their own potential and to contribute meaningfully to the collective well-being of society.

In Dr. Minakshi Bansal, we find a remarkable synthesis of the artist, the scholar, the healer, and the social activist. Her life's work stands as a beacon of hope and a source of inspiration for individuals seeking to make a difference in the world. Her story is a compelling reminder of the power of individual action, rooted in compassion and driven by a profound commitment to the betterment of humanity. Dr. Minakshi's legacy is not just in the tangible outcomes of her efforts but in the enduring spirit of inquiry, empathy, and service that she embodies.

Preface

In this book, we embark on a journey through the complex and transformative world of emotional intelligence (EI) and its profound impact on child development. Emotional intelligence is more than just a set of skills; it is a fundamental aspect of human development that influences our ability to navigate the world with understanding, empathy, and effectiveness. Understanding and nurturing these skills from an early age is crucial, as it shapes the emotional and social fabric of our children's future.

The significance of emotional intelligence in the developmental stages of a child cannot be overstated. It is through the mastery of these skills that children learn to identify and manage their own emotions, understand and empathize with the emotions of others, and develop effective communication and social skills. These capabilities lay the groundwork for building relationships, solving problems, and managing conflicts—skills that are essential throughout life, from the playground to the boardroom.

Through the pages of this book, we explore the different components of emotional intelligence, including self-awareness, self-regulation, motivation, empathy, and social skills. Each component is dissected to understand its role in the broader context of daily activities and interactions. This exploration is not just theoretical but is packed with practical guidance, real-life examples, and direct strategies to foster these skills. Parents, educators, and anyone involved in child development will find invaluable resources here to help nurture a child's emotional intelligence.

The development of emotional intelligence begins the moment a child interacts with the world. From the first display of a toddler's empathy to the complex emotional negotiations of teenagers, each stage of a child's life offers unique challenges and opportunities for growth. This book provides a roadmap for navigating these stages, offering insights into how emotional intelligence can be integrated into everyday parenting and teaching practices.

Moreover, the role of the environment cannot be ignored in shaping a child's emotional intelligence. Family dynamics, educational settings, and broader societal influences all play pivotal roles in the emotional development of a child. We delve into how these factors can either support or hinder the development of emotional intelligence, providing a holistic view that acknowledges the complexity of real-world influences on a child's development.

As we progress through the book, we also confront the challenges and setbacks that are inherent in developing emotional intelligence. Not every child has the same starting point in their emotional education. Some face significant obstacles—from personal disabilities to challenging life circumstances. This book addresses these challenges head-on, offering specialized advice and adaptive strategies to meet the diverse needs of all children, ensuring that no child is left behind in the quest to develop emotional intelligence.

The journey of developing emotional intelligence is, indeed, a lifelong endeavor. As children grow into adults, the seeds of emotional intelligence sown during childhood bear fruit in the form of healthier relationships, improved mental health, and greater career success. This book not only focuses on childhood but also touches on how emotional intelligence evolves and continues to influence individuals into adulthood.

In writing this book, my goal has been to illuminate the path toward greater emotional intelligence in a way that is both scientifically grounded and accessible. The strategies and concepts discussed are designed to be actionable, enabling parents and educators to apply these ideas in practical, impactful ways. It is my hope that this book will serve as a valuable resource for those dedicated to nurturing the next generation of emotionally intelligent individuals.

The journey from 'feeling' to 'healing'—from experiencing raw emotions to understanding and managing them effectively—is a transformative process that begins in childhood but never truly ends. This book is a guide for all those committed to making this journey a successful one, filled with growth, learning, and, ultimately, a deeper understanding of what it means to be human.

Dr. Minakshi Bansal
Social Activist
Ahmedabad, Gujarat, Bharat

I
Understanding Emotional Intelligence

Emotional Intelligence (EI) is a profound framework that encompasses the ability to recognize, understand, manage, and utilize emotions effectively in oneself and others. In the context of child development, EI is not just a set of skills but a crucial pillar that supports a child's ability to navigate the social complexities of their world, adapt to changes, and foster positive relationships.

The concept of EI was popularized in the 1990s by psychologist Daniel Goleman, who identified it as a key factor in achieving personal and professional success. Since then, the idea has been expanded into educational settings with compelling evidence suggesting that children who develop strong emotional intelligence tend to have better overall mental health, higher academic performance, and stronger interpersonal relationships.

Foundational Aspects of Emotional Intelligence

At the heart of emotional intelligence are four primary skills: self-awareness, self-management, social awareness, and relationship management. Self-awareness involves understanding one's own emotions and how they affect thoughts and behavior. This is where emotional intelligence begins. For children, developing self-awareness can mean recognizing when they feel happy, sad, frustrated, or excited, and understanding that their feelings can influence their actions.

Following self-awareness is self-management, which is the ability to regulate one's emotions to handle impulses, maintain focus, and perform competently. In young children, self-management is crucial during interactions with peers, such as taking turns during playtime or managing frustration during learning activities.

Social awareness deals with the understanding of others' emotions, needs, and concerns. It helps children grasp social cues, such as body language and facial expressions, which are essential for developing empathy. By fostering social awareness, children learn to put themselves in others' shoes and understand diverse perspectives.

Finally, relationship management involves the skills necessary to make and maintain healthy relationships. It encompasses communicating clearly, listening actively, cooperating, resisting inappropriate social pressure, negotiating conflict constructively, and seeking help when needed. For children, this could mean learning to share, playing cooperatively, and developing friendships.

Relevance of EI in Early Childhood Development

The early years of a child's life are critical for emotional intelligence development. This period is marked by rapid growth in cognitive and social capabilities, making it an ideal time for foundational EI skills to be nurtured. Emotional intelligence in early childhood sets the stage for more complex skill development as children grow. It influences a variety of life outcomes, including social behaviors, learning abilities, and psychological well-being.

In educational settings, integrating EI can transform classrooms into emotionally supportive and enriching environments. Teachers and caregivers play a pivotal role in modeling emotional intelligence through their interactions with each other and with students. By embedding EI principles into daily routines and classroom activities, educators can promote an atmosphere of emotional awareness and mutual respect.

Impact of Emotional Intelligence on Child Development

The impact of developing strong emotional intelligence in childhood is profound and far-reaching. Children with high EI are better equipped to handle interpersonal relationships and conflicts, perform better academically, and exhibit healthier responses to stress and adversity.

Academically, students with high emotional intelligence often have better concentration, which directly correlates with higher academic achievements. They tend to have better problem-solving skills because they can manage their emotions during challenging tasks. Additionally, emotionally intelligent children are more adaptable to different learning environments and can navigate social challenges with peers more effectively.

From a psychological perspective, children who cultivate EI early on tend to have a lower incidence of mental health issues. They are better at managing stress and rebounding from negative experiences. This resilience not only helps them during their school years but well into adulthood.

Cultivating Emotional Intelligence

Cultivating emotional intelligence in children requires consistent effort from parents, educators, and the community. It involves teaching kids to communicate their feelings effectively, to recognize others' emotions, to resolve conflicts constructively, and to develop a strong sense of self-awareness and empathy.

Activities such as reading stories with emotional content, engaging in play that involves turn-taking and role-playing, and openly discussing emotions and how they affect us, are all effective ways to foster EI. Moreover, creating an environment where emotions are openly discussed and not judged is crucial in teaching children that feelings are a natural part of human experience.

The development of emotional intelligence is an indispensable component of child development. Its influence spans the cognitive, social, and emotional domains, providing children with a robust foundation for understanding themselves and others. By prioritizing emotional intelligence from an early age, we pave the way for our children to become empathetic, successful, and psychologically resilient individuals. Through conscious efforts at home and in educational settings, we can nurture a generation that is not only smart but also emotionally intelligent, equipped to face the complexities of the world with competence and confidence.

"Emotional intelligence begins in the small
moments of listening and understanding, allowing
us to build bridges of empathy that stretch across
even the widest gaps of our differences."

ം

II

The Building Blocks of EI in Early Childhood

Emotional intelligence (EI) in early childhood is a cornerstone for lifelong mental health and social success. Understanding and fostering the foundational emotions in young children not only prepares them for future challenges but also equips them with the tools necessary for emotional well-being and interpersonal effectiveness. The exploration of these foundational emotions—joy, sadness, fear, anger, and surprise—provides a blueprint for how children perceive and interact with the world.

Foundational Emotions Defined

The concept of foundational emotions refers to the basic emotions that are universally recognized and experienced by humans from a very early age. These emotions are often instinctive and serve as the first layer of emotional skills that children develop. Recognizing and managing these basic emotions are the first steps in building emotional intelligence.

Joy: This is one of the first emotions a child expresses and learns to recognize. It is associated with an environment of safety, love, and encouragement. The expression of joy through smiles, laughter, and excitement is crucial as it reinforces behaviors and experiences that are positive.

Sadness: Unlike joy, sadness is a reflective emotion that often helps children understand more complex feelings. It can stem from experiences of loss or disappointment. Teaching children to express sadness appropriately and to manage it effectively is vital for their emotional development.

Fear: This emotion is protective in nature but can become problematic if not properly managed. Early childhood often involves encountering new experiences that can trigger fear. Helping children understand and cope with fear supports their ability to face new challenges confidently as they grow.

Anger: While often viewed negatively, anger is a natural response to perceived threats or injustices. It is crucial for children to learn how to express anger in a healthy way, understanding that it is a normal emotion that can be managed and channeled into positive outcomes.

Surprise: This emotion is linked to unexpected events, which can be pleasant or unpleasant. Surprise can help children learn to adapt to new situations and is closely tied to curiosity and learning.

Expression of Emotions in Young Children

The way young children express these emotions can significantly influence their development of emotional intelligence. It is through the expression and recognition of emotions that children begin to build empathy and understand social cues. Parents and caregivers play a critical role in this aspect by validating children's feelings and modeling appropriate emotional responses.

Emotional expression in young children is often more visceral and less filtered than in adults. Children might scream out of excitement or cry loudly when upset. These expressions are natural and should be addressed with understanding rather than suppression. Encouraging children to express their emotions freely and appropriately is a fundamental step in helping them develop EI.

Impact of Emotional Development on Early Learning

Developing emotional intelligence in early childhood is intricately linked to cognitive and social development. Children who are adept at recognizing and managing their emotions are generally more successful in social interactions and academic settings. They tend to have better concentration, are more receptive to learning, and can resolve conflicts with peers more effectively.

In educational environments, children with a strong foundation in emotional intelligence are often more engaged and can navigate the challenges of early schooling with greater ease. They are also better at handling the stress and anxiety that can come with new academic challenges.

Nurturing Emotional Intelligence through Play

Play is an essential tool in nurturing emotional intelligence. Through play, children learn to cooperate, resolve conflicts, and express themselves. Role-playing games, for instance, allow children to experiment with different emotional roles and outcomes, teaching them empathy and improving their ability to read emotional cues in others.

Furthermore, play provides a safe space for children to explore their emotions and the emotions of others. It fosters creativity, which is closely linked to emotional flexibility—a key component of emotional intelligence. Engaging children in play that stimulates emotional and social learning is an effective strategy for early childhood educators and parents alike.

The early years are critical for setting the foundations of emotional intelligence. By focusing on the basic emotions and their appropriate expression, we can equip children with the skills needed to navigate their emotional landscapes and interpersonal relationships effectively. This foundational work not only benefits individual children but also creates a more emotionally intelligent and compassionate society. As we continue to uncover the complexities of emotional development, it remains clear that the journey of emotional intelligence begins in the very early stages of life, with profound implications for personal and collective well-being.

The ability to navigate emotions is not just about managing the storms within but also about recognizing the calm in others, fostering connections that are deep and genuine."

৪৩

III

The Heart of Emotional Intelligence

Empathy stands as a central pillar in the development of emotional intelligence (EI), particularly because it directly influences how individuals connect with and understand others around them. It extends beyond mere emotional awareness to include an active engagement with the feelings of others, encompassing both emotional and cognitive aspects. Understanding the development of empathy and its profound impact on social interactions is crucial in early childhood, as it sets the stage for richer interpersonal relationships and a more compassionate society.

The Dual Aspects of Empathy

Empathy involves two primary components: affective empathy and cognitive empathy. Affective empathy refers to the ability to share the feelings of another person, feeling what they feel as they experience emotions. This kind of empathy can be seen in young children when they react to another child's distress by crying themselves or by showing concern. Cognitive empathy, on the other hand, involves understanding another person's perspective or mental state, which is crucial for developing social skills and moral reasoning.

Both aspects of empathy are essential for emotional intelligence, as they enhance an individual's capacity to navigate social complexities with sensitivity and awareness. For young children, these skills are foundational, forming the basis for more complex social interactions as they grow.

Development of Empathy in Early Childhood

Empathy begins to develop from a very young age. Infants display primitive forms of empathy when they respond to the emotional expressions of others, especially their primary caregivers. As children grow, their empathetic abilities mature through their interactions and through the nurturing they receive. By the age of two, most children can exhibit basic empathetic behaviors, such as comforting a distressed playmate or showing concern for a hurt parent.

The development of empathy is significantly influenced by the environment in which a child is raised. Children learn empathy largely by observing and mimicking the behavior of adults. Parents and caregivers who express empathetic and compassionate behavior encourage similar responses in children. For example, a parent who shows understanding and patience in the face of a child's frustration teaches the child to respond similarly to others' frustrations.

The Role of Empathy in Social Interactions

Empathy is fundamental to successful social interactions. It enables individuals to form connections, build friendships, and maintain healthy relationships. In the context of early childhood, the development of empathy is closely linked to the ability to play cooperatively, share, and take turns—all of which are crucial for positive social experiences.

Children who are empathetic are generally more popular among their peers and are better able to handle conflicts constructively. They are less likely to engage in bullying behaviors and are more likely to exhibit prosocial behaviors such as helping, sharing, and comforting others. Empathy thus not only benefits the individual child but also enhances the social environment, making it more nurturing and supportive.

Empathy and Emotional Regulation

Another significant aspect of empathy in the development of emotional intelligence is its impact on emotional regulation. Empathy encourages not only understanding and sharing the emotions of others but also necessitates a certain level of emotional control. For instance, to comfort a friend, a child must first manage their own emotional response to the friend's distress.

This regulation is critical for emotional maturity and is a skill that children continue to refine well into adulthood. By learning to regulate their emotions, children can respond more appropriately and sensitively to social cues, enhancing their interactions and relationships.

Nurturing Empathy in Children

Fostering empathy in children is a proactive process that involves several strategies. Storytelling and role-playing can be particularly effective, as they allow children to step into another's shoes and view situations from different perspectives. Additionally, discussing emotions openly and teaching children to label their feelings accurately helps them better understand and connect with the emotions of others.

Parents and educators play a crucial role in modeling empathetic behavior. By responding to children's needs with understanding and care, adults demonstrate empathy in action, providing a blueprint for children to follow. Furthermore, creating an environment where emotions are respected and valued promotes empathy by encouraging children to express and manage their feelings constructively.

Empathy is indeed the heart of emotional intelligence. Its development from an early age is essential for nurturing emotionally intelligent, compassionate individuals who can contribute positively to their social worlds. Through deliberate teaching and modeling of empathetic behaviors, we can equip children with the skills necessary to understand and connect with others deeply and authentically, enriching their lives and the communities they are part of. This foundational skill not only fosters personal growth and happiness but also holds the potential to shape a more empathetic and understanding society.

"*Resilience is more than recovering from a fall; it is about learning the art of bouncing back stronger, with lessons learned and wisdom gained.*"

⚮

IV
Emotional Regulation in Toddlers

Emotional regulation is a crucial aspect of early development, especially during the toddler years when children experience rapid emotional and physical growth. This stage marks a critical period for establishing patterns that affect how children manage their emotions throughout their lives. Effective emotional regulation involves recognizing emotions, understanding how to respond to them, and learning techniques to manage feelings appropriately. For toddlers, these skills are foundational, setting the stage for future emotional intelligence.

Understanding Emotional Regulation in Toddlers

Emotional regulation refers to the process by which individuals influence which emotions they have, when they have them, and how they experience and express these emotions. In toddlers, emotional regulation is still in a primitive stage. Toddlers often experience intense emotions and may express these feelings through crying, tantrums, or laughter. These expressions are not only normal but necessary for their emotional development.

The ability of toddlers to regulate their emotions is closely linked to their overall emotional and cognitive development. As they grow, they begin to understand more about their feelings and how to handle them. This development is influenced significantly by their environment and the emotional modeling they receive from adults.

Strategies for Enhancing Emotional Regulation

Helping toddlers develop emotional regulation involves several key strategies that parents and caregivers can employ:

Modeling Calm Behavior: Children learn how to handle emotions largely by observing those around them. When parents and caregivers consistently model calmness and emotional control, toddlers learn to mimic these behaviors. Demonstrating healthy ways to express anger, sadness, or frustration helps toddlers understand that while emotions are natural, they can be managed.

Talking About Emotions: Even at a young age, children benefit from having their feelings articulated. Using simple language to describe and label emotions helps toddlers make sense of what they are feeling. For example, saying, "I see that you are upset because your toy broke," helps the child recognize the emotion of sadness or frustration and understand its cause.

Creating a Supportive Environment: A stable and supportive environment is crucial for helping toddlers learn to regulate their emotions. This means not only physical safety but also emotional security. Toddlers who feel secure are more likely to explore their emotions in healthy ways and learn to manage them effectively.

Using Tools and Toys: Various tools can aid in teaching emotional regulation. Toys that involve turn-taking can teach patience, while stuffed animals or dolls can be used in role-playing exercises to practice expressing and managing emotions. Additionally, sensory toys like stress balls or fidget spinners can help manage feelings of anxiety or agitation.

Establishing Routines: Routines provide a sense of predictability that can be calming to toddlers. A regular schedule for meals, naps, and playtime helps reduce anxiety and manageability, making emotional regulation easier.

Encouraging Expression Through Art: Artistic activities provide an outlet for expressing emotions. Drawing, painting, or playing with clay allows toddlers to express their feelings in a safe and manageable way. These activities also offer opportunities for discussing emotions and reinforcing emotional language.

Practicing Mindfulness and Relaxation Techniques: Simple mindfulness exercises can be adapted for toddlers, such as deep breathing with blowing bubbles or lying down with a teddy bear on their stomach to watch it rise and fall with their breath. These techniques teach toddlers how to calm themselves.

Positive Reinforcement: Praising toddlers when they successfully manage their emotions reinforces positive behavior and encourages them to handle their emotions constructively in the future. Positive reinforcement can be as simple as a hug or verbal praise.

The Role of Caregivers and Educators

The role of caregivers and educators in teaching emotional regulation cannot be overstated. Consistent, responsive caregiving—where adults promptly and effectively address a toddler's emotional needs—helps build the skills necessary for emotional regulation. Educators in daycare and preschool settings can incorporate lessons and activities that foster emotional understanding and regulation, creating a community that supports each child's emotional growth.

Emotional regulation is a key skill that toddlers need to develop during their early years. By employing effective techniques and strategies, caregivers can help children learn how to handle their emotions in healthy ways. This skill set not only benefits the toddler during the early years but lays the foundation for their lifelong emotional intelligence, social interactions, and personal well-being. Fostering these skills early in life ensures that children grow into adults who are well-equipped to manage their emotions, face challenges, and engage positively with the world around them.

"True emotional growth is seeing every experience, good or bad, as a stepping stone to a greater understanding of oneself and the world around us."

৪৩

V

The Role of Parents and Caregivers

Parents and caregivers play an indispensable role in the emotional development of children. Their influence extends beyond the basic needs of safety and nourishment to encompass the nurturing of emotional intelligence (EI). By actively engaging in their child's emotional education, parents and caregivers lay the foundation for lifelong skills in empathy, emotional regulation, and interpersonal relationships. Effective guidance on nurturing EI at home involves a combination of understanding, patience, consistent modeling, and deliberate teaching of emotional skills.

Understanding Emotional Intelligence at Home

The first step in nurturing emotional intelligence in children is for parents and caregivers to have a clear understanding of what EI entails. Emotional intelligence involves the ability to recognize one's own emotions and those of others, to differentiate between different feelings, and to use this emotional information to guide thinking and behavior. It also involves managing emotions to adapt to environments or achieve one's goals. At home, this means creating an environment where emotions are openly discussed, and emotional expressions are both allowed and respected.

Creating an Emotionally Rich Environment

An emotionally rich environment is one where feelings are freely expressed and respected. Parents and caregivers can foster such an environment by being emotionally open themselves. Showing a range of emotions in a healthy way allows children to learn that feelings are a normal part of life. Discussing emotions as they arise in daily situations provides context to the emotional landscape, helping children understand how and why emotions occur.

Modeling Emotional Intelligence

Children learn a great deal by observing the behaviors of adults. Parents and caregivers who demonstrate emotional intelligence in their actions naturally teach these skills to their children. This includes showing empathy to others, managing one's own emotions effectively, and communicating feelings appropriately. For example, a parent who expresses frustration in a calm and constructive manner provides a powerful lesson in emotional regulation.

Effective Communication

Central to nurturing emotional intelligence is effective communication. This not only involves talking about feelings but also listening actively to what children have to say. Parents should encourage children to express their emotions verbally, using age-appropriate language, and show that they value what the child feels and says. This practice builds a child's confidence in their emotional expressions and aids in their emotional development.

Teaching Emotional Skills

Apart from modeling emotional skills, direct teaching is also essential. This can be done through everyday interactions as well as during specific teaching moments. Techniques include:

Naming Emotions: Help children develop an emotional vocabulary by naming emotions as they occur. This teaches children to identify and label their feelings, a fundamental aspect of emotional intelligence.

Discussing Causes and Effects of Emotions: Engage in discussions about what causes certain emotions and what effects they can have on oneself and others. This builds emotional awareness and empathy.

Problem Solving: When emotional problems arise, such as conflicts with siblings or friends, guide children through the problem-solving process. Discuss various emotional responses and their consequences, and encourage children to come up with solutions that consider everyone's feelings.

Setting the Example with Emotional Regulation

Parents and caregivers are often the primary role models for emotional regulation. Demonstrating how to cope with stress in healthy ways, such as through exercise, reading, or hobbies, teaches children practical methods to handle their own emotions. Likewise, showing that it's okay to take a time-out when emotions become overwhelming can teach children valuable techniques for calming down.

Encouraging Empathy

Fostering empathy is another critical aspect of nurturing EI. This can be encouraged through activities that promote understanding and caring about others' feelings. Reading stories together, discussing the characters' emotions, and relating them to real-life situations can be very effective. Additionally, encouraging children to consider how their actions affect others helps deepen their sense of empathy.

Consistency and Patience

The journey of nurturing emotional intelligence is ongoing and requires consistency and patience. Emotional development can be complex and children will inevitably face challenges as they learn and grow. Consistent support and guidance from parents are crucial in helping them navigate this aspect of their development.

The role of parents and caregivers in nurturing emotional intelligence at home is multifaceted and profoundly important. It involves creating an emotionally aware environment, modeling emotional intelligence, teaching emotional skills, and providing consistent support. Through these efforts, parents and caregivers not only enhance their children's emotional capabilities but also contribute to their overall well-being and success in life. This foundational work not only benefits the child in their formative years but sets the stage for a lifetime of emotional health and intelligence.

"In the garden of the mind, empathy is the sunlight that encourages understanding to bloom, transforming seeds of perception into blossoms of connection."

&

VI

Emotional Intelligence in the Classroom

Integrating emotional intelligence (EI) into early education settings is a transformative approach that enhances not only the learning environment but also significantly contributes to the holistic development of young learners. By incorporating EI concepts into the curriculum, educators can equip children with essential skills that promote emotional well-being, improve social interactions, and boost academic achievement. This integration involves understanding the components of emotional intelligence, creating an emotionally supportive learning environment, and employing specific strategies and activities that foster emotional growth.

Foundations of Emotional Intelligence in Education

Emotional intelligence in education encompasses more than the mere recognition and management of one's emotions. It also involves empathy, social skills, motivation, and self-regulation. These elements are crucial in a classroom setting where children interact with peers and face various academic and social challenges. Educators who understand and value the importance of EI are better equipped to nurture these skills in children.

Creating an Emotionally Supportive Learning Environment

The first step in integrating EI into the classroom is to create an environment that supports emotional learning. This involves establishing a classroom culture where all emotions are acknowledged and respected. Teachers can set the tone by being emotionally available and responsive to students, demonstrating empathy, and handling conflicts and emotions in constructive ways.

Teachers should strive to build strong, personal connections with students, which can provide a secure base from which students feel comfortable exploring their emotions. Additionally, classroom rules and routines should support emotional safety, allowing students to express themselves without fear of judgment or ridicule.

Curriculum Integration

Integrating EI into the curriculum can be achieved through both explicit and implicit educational practices. Explicitly, emotional intelligence can be taught as a separate subject similar to how social studies or science is taught. This can include dedicated lessons on identifying emotions, understanding the reasons behind emotions, and learning how to manage them effectively.

Implicit integration involves incorporating emotional intelligence concepts into other subjects. For example, literature provides excellent opportunities to discuss characters' emotional experiences and choices, which can lead to deeper discussions about empathy and emotional responses. In science classes, discussions about human biology can include aspects of how emotions affect our bodies.

Activities to Foster Emotional Intelligence

Numerous activities can be employed in early education settings to enhance emotional intelligence:

Role-Playing and Social Stories: These are effective tools for teaching problem-solving, empathy, and perspective-taking. Children can act out various social situations and explore different emotional outcomes based on their actions.

Emotion Corners: Designating a specific area in the classroom where children can go to deal with overwhelming emotions can be beneficial. This space could include comforting items, emotion cards, and resources to help them process their feelings and come back to class ready to learn.

Daily Check-Ins: Starting the day with a mood check-in helps children become more aware of their feelings and the feelings of their peers. This can be as simple as having a chart where students place a marker next to an emoji that represents their current mood.

Mindfulness and Relaxation Techniques: Teaching children basic mindfulness practices such as deep breathing, meditation, or guided imagery can help improve their concentration and emotional regulation. These techniques can be incorporated into the daily schedule to help set a calm, focused tone for the day.

Teacher Training and Professional Development

For EI to be effectively integrated into the classroom, teachers themselves need to be trained in emotional intelligence. Professional development workshops can provide educators with the skills necessary to understand and teach EI concepts. These training sessions can also offer strategies for teachers to manage their own emotions in the classroom setting—a key aspect of modeling emotional intelligence.

Assessment and Reflection

Assessing the impact of EI integration in the classroom is vital. Educators can use informal assessments, such as observations and student feedback, to gauge the effectiveness of EI activities. Reflecting on what works and what doesn't allows teachers to adjust their approaches to better meet the emotional needs of their students.

Integrating emotional intelligence into early education settings requires a thoughtful and comprehensive approach that includes modifying the learning environment, curriculum, and teaching practices. By doing so, educators not only enhance the educational experience but also support the emotional and social development of their students. This holistic approach prepares children not just for academic success but for lifelong personal and professional achievements, nurturing a generation of emotionally intelligent and socially responsible individuals.

"When children learn to manage their emotions effectively, they are not just navigating their childhood better; they are setting the sails for a successful adulthood."

ꝏ

VII
Play and Emotional Learning

Play is a fundamental aspect of childhood, serving not only as a source of joy and entertainment but also as a critical medium for emotional and social learning. Through play, children explore the world, experiment with social roles, express their thoughts and emotions, and learn to manage complex interpersonal interactions. This natural activity offers an invaluable opportunity to teach and enhance emotional skills in a relaxed and engaging environment.

Understanding the Role of Play in Emotional Development

Play is intrinsically linked to the development of emotional intelligence. It provides a safe space for children to express feelings, try out new emotional behaviors, and learn from their experiences without serious repercussions. During play, children often mimic adult behaviors, which helps them understand and assimilate social norms and emotional responses. This role-playing is crucial as it allows children to experiment with different emotional states and outcomes, enhancing their understanding of emotional dynamics in a controlled environment.

Types of Play and Their Impact on Emotional Skills

Different types of play contribute to the development of various emotional skills:

Free Play: This unstructured play allows children to make their own decisions and explore their interests. It fosters independence, creativity, and emotional expression. Children learn to negotiate, cooperate, and solve conflicts with peers, which are essential components of emotional intelligence.

Guided Play: Guided play, which involves more direction and input from adults, can be used to introduce specific emotional learning concepts. For example, a teacher might use a puppet show to demonstrate how to resolve a common conflict or to show empathy towards others.

Physical Play: Activities like running, jumping, and other sports help children manage energy levels and emotions such as excitement, frustration, and anger. Learning to regulate these emotions in play can translate into better emotional regulation in more formal or stressful situations.

Creative Play: Drawing, music, and drama provide outlets for children to express and manage their emotions. These activities encourage children to delve into their feelings and can be particularly therapeutic for children who might struggle with verbal expression.

Strategies for Integrating Emotional Learning into Play

To maximize the benefits of play in emotional learning, specific strategies can be employed:

Setting Emotional Learning Goals for Play Activities: Educators and parents can set objectives for play, such as learning to take turns, expressing feelings using words, or helping others who are in distress. Clear goals help guide the child's actions and reflections during play.

Reflecting on Play Experiences: After play sessions, discussing what happened during play can reinforce learning. Asking questions like, "How did you feel when that happened?" or "What could you do differently next time?" helps children understand the emotional consequences of their actions.

Using Emotional Vocabulary: During play, use specific emotional words to describe what the child or characters in the play might be feeling. This vocabulary building is crucial for emotional development as it gives children the language needed to express their feelings more accurately.

Modeling Positive Emotional Responses: During interactive play, adults can model how to respond to various situations with emotional intelligence. For example, showing patience and humor in the face of challenges or expressing joy at a play partner's success can teach children appropriate emotional reactions.

Encouraging Cooperative Play: Activities that require children to work together toward a common goal can teach empathy and perspective-taking. These are key aspects of emotional intelligence that help children understand and relate to the emotions of others.

The Benefits of Play in Emotional Learning

The benefits of integrating play into emotional learning are extensive. Play helps children learn to control their emotions and impulses, develop empathy, improve their communication skills, and gain self-confidence. These skills are not only crucial for personal happiness and success but also form the foundation for healthy social relationships.

Moreover, play is a dynamic and adaptable tool. It can be tailored to the individual emotional needs of each child, making it possible to support a wide range of emotional competencies from a very young age.

Play is not just a way for children to spend energy and have fun; it is also an essential part of their emotional education. By using play as a tool to teach and enhance emotional skills, parents and educators can provide children with the experiences necessary to develop strong emotional intelligence. This preparation in early childhood sets the groundwork for their ability to handle future emotional challenges more effectively, promoting overall well-being and success throughout their lives.

"Every act of listening is a stepping-stone towards understanding, and every moment of understanding is a leap towards empathy."

୫୬

VIII

Friendships and Emotional Growth

Friendships during childhood play a pivotal role in emotional growth and development. These relationships provide a context for children to practice social skills, express emotions, and navigate the complexities of interpersonal interactions. The impact of friendships extends beyond mere companionship, influencing emotional regulation, empathy, self-esteem, and a myriad of other emotional competencies essential for personal and social functioning.

The Role of Friendships in Emotional Development

Friendships serve as an important training ground for developing a range of emotional skills. Through interactions with peers, children learn to negotiate, share, resolve conflicts, and experience a range of emotions such as joy, disappointment, jealousy, and forgiveness. These experiences are crucial as they help children understand themselves and others, fostering emotional intelligence that is vital for their lifelong mental health and well-being.

Navigating Emotions Through Friendships

One of the first emotional lessons from friendships is the management of one's feelings. Friendships require children to regulate their emotions to maintain harmony and enjoy their time together. For instance, when disputes arise, children must learn to handle anger or frustration constructively to restore peace or come to a compromise. Such interactions enhance emotional regulation skills, teaching children when and how to express their feelings.

Empathy and Understanding

Friendships also cultivate empathy. Regular interactions with peers make children more attuned to the feelings and needs of others. By observing and engaging with friends who may react differently to similar situations, children learn that the emotional responses of individuals can vary widely and that these responses are deeply influenced by personal feelings and experiences. This awareness is the foundation of empathy, which is essential for the development of sensitive and caring interpersonal relationships.

Self-Esteem and Confidence

Having friends can significantly boost a child's self-esteem and confidence. Friendships provide a sense of belonging and acceptance that is crucial during childhood, a period often marked by self-discovery and seeking one's place in the social world. Positive feedback and support from peers reinforce a child's sense of self-worth and contribute to a healthier self-image.

Social Skills and Cooperation

The cooperative aspects of play and shared activities within friendships teach children valuable social skills such as taking turns, cooperating towards common goals, and supporting one another. These skills are not only essential for current social interactions but also for future professional relationships and personal relationships in adulthood.

Resilience Through Emotional Support

Friendships provide emotional support that helps children cope with various stressors, whether these are academic pressures, family issues, or personal challenges. The support network that friends provide acts as a buffer against psychological stress, enhancing resilience. This emotional backing is crucial, particularly when children face life's challenges, as it gives them the strength and reassurance that they are not alone.

Handling Negative Experiences

While friendships can be a source of joy and growth, they can also involve negative experiences such as conflicts, misunderstandings, and the pain of rejection or betrayal. Navigating these challenges is a critical part of emotional learning. Through such experiences, children learn to deal with loss, forgive, and sometimes, reconcile. The coping mechanisms they develop from dealing with friendship troubles can serve them throughout life.

Encouraging Positive Friendships

Given the importance of friendships in emotional development, it is beneficial for parents and educators to encourage positive social interactions. This can be done by creating social opportunities through group activities, guiding children on how to be good friends, and discussing values like empathy, respect, and kindness. Monitoring for signs of unhealthy relationships or bullying is also crucial and requires timely adult intervention to prevent negative emotional outcomes.

Reflection and Growth

As children grow, their friendships often become more complex and emotionally significant. Encouraging children to reflect on their interactions and understand the qualities that make friendships rewarding or challenging can foster greater emotional intelligence. Discussions about friendships can help children consider not just how they are influenced by others, but also how they influence others' emotions, leading to more mindful and empathetic social interactions.

Friendships are integral to a child's emotional and social development. They provide a complex interplay of challenges and rewards that foster growth and learning. By navigating the emotional ups and downs of friendships, children develop a richer emotional intelligence that prepares them for the complexities of adult relationships. Therefore, understanding and supporting the development of healthy friendships during childhood is essential for nurturing emotionally intelligent, resilient, and socially adept individuals.

"The strongest leaders are those who have mastered not the command of others, but the understanding of themselves."

༄

IX

The Impact of Technology on Emotional Skills

In today's digital age, technology plays a significant role in the lives of children, influencing their emotional and social development in profound ways. While technology offers numerous educational and social benefits, it also presents challenges to emotional skills and social interactions. Balancing technology use with emotional and social learning is crucial for ensuring that children develop healthy emotional habits and the ability to engage effectively with others.

Understanding the Influence of Technology

Technology's influence on emotional development starts from a very young age, as children are increasingly exposed to screens in the form of tablets, smartphones, and televisions. These digital tools provide unique opportunities for learning and entertainment but also pose risks if not managed properly. Excessive or unmonitored use of technology can lead to issues such as reduced face-to-face interactions, diminished physical activity, and overreliance on digital communication.

Benefits of Technology in Emotional and Social Learning

Technology, when used appropriately, can support emotional and social learning. Educational apps and games can teach children about emotions, empathy, and social skills through interactive and engaging platforms. Additionally, technology connects children with peers and family members across distances, facilitating social interactions and maintaining relationships that might not otherwise be possible. For instance, video calls can help children stay connected with family members who live far away, reinforcing familial bonds and providing emotional support.

Challenges Posed by Technology

Despite its benefits, the pervasive presence of technology can disrupt the natural development of emotional and social skills. One significant concern is that screen time often replaces time spent on direct human interactions, which are essential for learning social cues, facial expressions, and the nuances of human emotions. Moreover, digital communication, while convenient, typically lacks the emotional depth of face-to-face interactions and can lead to misunderstandings and a decrease in empathy.

The instant gratification provided by technology can also impact emotional regulation. Children accustomed to immediate responses through digital interactions may find it challenging to develop patience and resilience when immediate outcomes are not possible. This can affect their ability to cope with frustration and delay gratification, which are critical components of emotional maturity.

Balancing Technology with Emotional Learning

To counteract the potential negative effects of technology on emotional development, a balanced approach is necessary. Parents and educators can implement strategies to ensure technology serves as a tool for enhancing, rather than hindering, emotional and social learning.

Set Boundaries on Screen Time: Establishing limits on the amount of time spent on screens is crucial. Encourage children to engage in offline activities that promote physical movement and face-to-face interactions.

Promote Quality Content: Choose apps, games, and digital media that are educational and promote social and emotional skills. Quality content should be age-appropriate and should ideally be used as a complement to, rather than a replacement for, real-world experiences.

Interactive Technology Use: Encourage interactive use of technology that involves parents or peers. Activities such as playing educational video games together or participating in family video chats can enhance social interactions and emotional engagement.

Teach Critical Thinking: As children interact with information and people online, it's important to teach them critical thinking skills. Discuss the content they view and teach them to question and analyze information critically.

Encourage Emotional Reflection: After using technology, encourage children to reflect on their emotional responses to what they saw or experienced online. This can include discussing how certain games or videos made them feel and why.

Model Balanced Use: Parents and educators should model balanced use of technology. Showing children that it's important to put away devices during meals or social interactions can teach them the value of undivided attention and presence in the moment.

Monitoring and Adapting Technology Use

Ongoing monitoring and adaptation of technology use are necessary as children grow and their needs change. Regular discussions about the role of technology, its benefits, and its limits can help children develop a healthy relationship with digital devices. As they mature, they can be more involved in setting their own boundaries and making choices about how they use technology.

Technology is an integral part of modern life and, when used wisely, can support emotional and social development in children. Balancing technology use with traditional emotional and social learning activities is essential to ensure children develop robust emotional intelligence and the social skills necessary to navigate both the virtual and real worlds. By adopting a thoughtful approach to technology use, parents and educators can help children harness the benefits of digital tools while mitigating their potential drawbacks.

"Conflict is not just an obstacle; when navigated
with emotional intelligence, it becomes a classroom
where the most valuable lessons of life are learned."

X

Understanding and Handling Anger

Anger is a natural and often misunderstood emotion that can be challenging for children to manage. Recognizing and dealing with anger effectively is crucial for children's emotional health and social development. Developing strategies to handle anger in healthy ways helps children build resilience, improve communication skills, and foster better relationships. This guidance is essential not just for immediate situations but also for their long-term emotional development.

The Nature of Anger in Children

Anger in children, much like in adults, is a normal emotional response to feeling frustrated, hurt, or powerless. It can arise from a variety of situations—conflicts with peers, unmet expectations, or even internal struggles such as difficulty with schoolwork. Understanding that anger itself is not negative is crucial; rather, it's how we handle and express anger that can lead to positive or negative outcomes.

For children, the expression of anger can range from mild irritation to intense rage. Young children, in particular, may have tantrums as they experience overwhelming feelings they don't yet have the skills to manage. As children grow, they start to learn more about the nuances of expressing their emotions, including anger.

Strategies for Managing Anger

Developing effective strategies for managing anger is crucial in helping children learn to handle their emotions constructively. These strategies can be cultivated at home and in educational settings:

Recognizing Anger Cues: Teaching children to recognize the signs of anger in themselves is the first step in managing this emotion. Physical cues such as clenched fists, a fast heartbeat, or feeling hot can alert a child that they are becoming angry. Recognizing these signs early can help them take steps to calm down before their feelings escalate.

Using Words to Express Anger: Children should be encouraged to verbalize their anger using words rather than aggressive actions. Teaching phrases such as "I am angry because..." helps children communicate their feelings clearly and directly without resorting to physical expressions of anger.

Teaching Deep Breathing and Counting Techniques: Simple relaxation techniques can be highly effective in calming down. Teaching children to take deep breaths, count to ten, or slowly count backwards from 20 can help mitigate the intensity of their anger, providing a pause that allows them to respond more thoughtfully.

Creating an Anger Plan: Just as schools conduct fire drills to prepare for emergencies, creating an 'anger drill' or plan can prepare children to deal with anger. An anger plan might include steps like identifying when they feel angry, using a calming technique, finding an adult to talk to, and thinking of solutions.

Encouraging Physical Activity: Physical activity is a great way for children to manage emotions, including anger. Activities like running, jumping, or even stomping can help release the buildup of stress and anger in a controlled and safe manner.

Providing Quiet Time or a Safe Space: Sometimes, the best way for a child to handle anger is to withdraw to a quiet place to cool down. Having a designated safe space, whether at home or school, where children can go to feel calm, can be incredibly beneficial.

Modeling Healthy Anger Management: Children learn a lot from observing adults. When parents, teachers, and other caregivers manage their own anger in healthy ways, they set a powerful example for children. Demonstrating techniques like discussing feelings calmly, walking away to cool down, or using humor to lighten the mood can teach children effective strategies for managing their own anger.

Problem-Solving Skills: Teaching children problem-solving skills helps them address the situations that may trigger anger. Discussing different scenarios and possible solutions can empower children to handle conflicts and frustrating situations more effectively.

Use of Art and Writing: Expressive activities such as drawing, painting, or writing stories can be therapeutic for children dealing with anger. These activities offer a safe outlet for expressing feelings and can help children make sense of their emotions.

Encouraging Reflection on Anger Experiences

After an anger episode, it's helpful for children to reflect on the experience. Discussing what triggered the anger, how they handled it, what they did well, and what they could do differently next time fosters self-awareness and learning. These reflections can be guided by adults in supportive ways, emphasizing learning and growth rather than punishment or criticism.

Understanding and managing anger effectively is critical for children's emotional development. By learning and practicing healthy anger management strategies, children gain essential skills that contribute to their emotional intelligence, enhance their interpersonal relationships, and enable them to navigate life's challenges more effectively. Encouraging children to handle anger constructively is an ongoing process that requires patience, practice, and support from the adults in their lives. Through these efforts, children can grow into emotionally healthy adults who understand how to express and manage their feelings in positive ways.

"Teaching a child to embrace their emotions with
intelligence is like planting a tree; it grows roots of
confidence that will anchor them throughout life."

☙

XI

Overcoming Fear and Anxiety

Fear and anxiety are common experiences in childhood, often manifesting as part of the normal development process as children learn to navigate the world around them. However, when these emotions become overwhelming or chronic, they can impede a child's ability to function and enjoy life. Helping children understand and cope with their fears and anxieties is crucial for their emotional resilience and well-being. Effective strategies can aid children in managing these feelings, ensuring they grow into confident and capable individuals.

Understanding Fear and Anxiety in Children

Fear is an emotional response to an immediate threat and is typically specific and short-lived. Anxiety, however, involves anticipation of future danger or problems, often leading to prolonged periods of distress. Children may experience fear and anxiety in various situations, such as during separation from parents, when facing new social settings, or when dealing with academic pressures.

Recognizing the signs of fear and anxiety is the first step in helping children cope. These signs might include clinginess, avoidance, sleep disturbances, stomachaches, or changes in eating habits. Children might also express their worries through questions about what if scenarios that reveal an anxious mind.

Strategies for Managing Fear and Anxiety

Several strategies can be employed to help children manage their fears and anxieties effectively:

Education about Fear and Anxiety: Teaching children about the nature of fear and anxiety can demystify these feelings and reduce their intensity. Explain that fear is a normal and natural response that everyone experiences and that anxiety is the body's way of alerting us to potential dangers, which sometimes gets overly protective.

Encouraging Open Communication: Create an environment where children feel safe to express their fears and anxieties without judgment. This support can significantly lessen the burden of these emotions. Listen attentively, acknowledge their feelings, and validate their experiences.

Developing Coping Skills: Teach children practical techniques to manage anxiety, such as deep breathing, meditation, or using visualization strategies to imagine themselves successfully facing their fears. Guided relaxation can also be a powerful tool in calming the mind and body.

Gradual Exposure: Gradually exposing children to the things they fear, in a controlled and supportive way, can significantly reduce the fear response. This approach, known as desensitization, helps children build confidence and reduce anxiety in a step-by-step manner.

Routine and Predictability: Maintaining a regular routine can provide a sense of security and predictability that helps alleviate anxiety. Structured daily activities that include time for play, relaxation, and sleep are essential for emotional stability.

Problem-Solving Skills: Encourage children to identify what triggers their anxiety and work together to find solutions or coping strategies. This empowerment helps reduce feelings of helplessness that often accompany anxiety.

Positive Reinforcement: Acknowledge and praise children when they manage their anxiety or face a fear. Positive reinforcement encourages them to continue using the strategies they have learned and to face their fears more confidently.

Modeling Healthy Behavior: Children learn a great deal from observing how adults manage stress and anxiety. By demonstrating healthy coping mechanisms, adults can provide a role model for managing difficult emotions.

Use of Stories and Books: Reading books that address fear and anxiety can help children understand and relate to these emotions. Stories in which characters overcome fears can provide both comfort and a framework for dealing with similar situations.

Professional Help: If a child's anxiety interferes with their daily life, seeking help from a pediatrician or a mental health professional can provide further guidance and support. Therapies such as cognitive-behavioral therapy are highly effective in treating anxiety disorders in children.

Supporting Emotional Growth

In addition to these strategies, fostering a general environment that promotes emotional growth is crucial. This environment should encourage resilience, where children learn that they can face challenges and emerge stronger. Activities that build self-esteem and a sense of accomplishment can also counteract the insecurities that often accompany anxiety.

Helping children overcome fear and anxiety involves a compassionate and proactive approach. By educating children about these emotions, encouraging them to express their feelings, teaching them practical coping strategies, and providing a stable environment, parents and educators can help children manage anxiety effectively. These efforts equip children with the tools they need to handle challenges throughout their lives, promoting not only their emotional health but also their overall well-being.

"Celebrating success should always be paired with embracing failure, for both teach invaluable lessons that lead to emotional maturity and resilience."

ജ

XII

Building Self-Esteem and Confidence

Building self-esteem and confidence in children is a vital aspect of their development, influencing their ability to face life's challenges with resilience and courage. Self-esteem refers to how much children value themselves and feel loved and accepted by others, while confidence is their belief in their own abilities. Encouraging a positive self-perception and confidence in children not only supports their current emotional and social engagement but also sets the groundwork for their future success and mental health.

Understanding Self-Esteem and Confidence

Self-esteem and confidence are closely intertwined; children with high self-esteem typically exhibit higher confidence, and vice versa. Self-esteem is developed from early childhood through the relationships children have with those around them and their early successes and failures. Confidence, meanwhile, is built through trying new things, overcoming challenges, and learning from both successes and failures.

Foundations of Building Self-Esteem and Confidence

Positive Affirmations and Praise: Regular, sincere praise for effort rather than outcome encourages children to value their work and persist despite setbacks. Positive affirmations can reinforce their belief in their abilities and inherent worth.

Setting Realistic Expectations: It's crucial for parents and educators to set achievable, age-appropriate expectations for children. Meeting these expectations can boost children's sense of accomplishment and self-esteem. Overly high expectations, however, may lead to feelings of inadequacy and lower self-esteem.

Encouraging Effort Over Results: Focusing on the effort children put into their activities rather than the outcome helps them develop a growth mindset. This mindset encourages them to see challenges as opportunities to learn and grow, which enhances their resilience and confidence.

Providing Opportunities for Success: Children build confidence by experiencing success. Providing them with opportunities to succeed in tasks that are suited to their skills and gradually increasing the difficulty can help build this confidence. Success in these endeavors reinforces their belief in their capabilities.

Modeling Positive Self-Talk: Children learn by observing the adults around them. When parents and teachers demonstrate positive self-talk and show confidence in their abilities, children are likely to emulate these attitudes.

Encouraging Independence and Responsibility: Allowing children to make choices and take on responsibilities appropriate for their age can significantly boost their confidence. Tasks like picking out their clothes, helping with household chores, or managing schoolwork provide them with opportunities to feel capable and competent.

Supportive Environment: Creating a supportive and loving environment where children feel safe expressing their thoughts and emotions without fear of judgment is essential for developing self-esteem. When children feel valued and accepted for who they are, their self-esteem flourishes.

Social Skills Development: Encouraging children to engage in social activities can enhance their social skills and improve their confidence in social settings. Skills like sharing, communicating clearly, and cooperating are developed through these interactions.

Handling Failures and Setbacks: Teaching children to handle failures and setbacks with resilience is crucial for building self-esteem and confidence. Helping them understand that failure is a normal part of learning and growth enables them to face challenges with a positive outlook.

Celebrating Uniqueness: Every child has unique talents and abilities. Recognizing and celebrating these individual differences can help children appreciate their own value and feel confident in their unique qualities.

Long-Term Impact of Self-Esteem and Confidence

Children with high self-esteem and confidence are more likely to engage in healthy behaviors, pursue their goals, and face new challenges with enthusiasm. They are also better equipped to handle peer pressure, make decisions independently, and navigate the complexities of social interactions.

Encouraging self-esteem and confidence in children is not about ensuring they are always happy or successful but about equipping them with the emotional tools they need to handle life's ups and downs. As they grow, these emotional foundations help them develop into well-rounded, resilient adults capable of managing their relationships and responsibilities effectively.

Building self-esteem and confidence in children requires consistent effort and a multifaceted approach, involving praise, realistic expectations, encouragement of effort, opportunities for success, and modeling of positive behaviors. By focusing on these areas, parents and educators can profoundly impact the emotional and psychological development of children, setting them on a path to becoming secure, competent, and confident individuals.

"Cultivating emotional intelligence is akin to crafting a lens that brings the world into clearer emotional focus, enhancing every interaction and decision."

ॐ

XIII

Conflict Resolution Skills

Teaching children to resolve conflicts amicably and effectively is a critical aspect of their social and emotional development. Conflict is a natural part of human relationships and learning to manage it at an early age can help children develop into well-adjusted adults with strong interpersonal skills. Effective conflict resolution fosters a sense of fairness, enhances communication skills, and promotes empathy, all of which are essential for healthy, lasting relationships.

Understanding Conflict in Childhood

Conflicts among children can arise over anything from sharing toys to differences in opinions and misunderstandings. The way these conflicts are handled can significantly impact a child's emotional and social growth. Children who learn to address conflicts constructively are likely to develop stronger friendships and perform better academically, as they are not bogged down by unresolved interpersonal issues.

Essential Conflict Resolution Skills

Several key skills form the basis of effective conflict resolution for children:

Identifying and Expressing Feelings: Teaching children to recognize and express their feelings clearly and respectfully is the first step in conflict resolution. When children can say, "I feel upset because I was left out of the game," instead of lashing out, it opens the door for understanding and dialogue.

Active Listening: Children need to learn to listen to others' perspectives without interrupting. Active listening also involves showing understanding through body language and verbal feedback, which confirms that the message has been received and understood.

Empathy: Understanding and relating to another's feelings can help in resolving conflicts. Empathy allows children to appreciate the other person's perspective, which can transform a confrontational situation into a cooperative endeavor.

Problem-Solving: Teaching children to come up with solutions that are acceptable to all parties involved encourages creative problem-solving and ensures that all voices are heard. This might involve compromise or finding a third option that satisfies everyone involved.

Assertiveness: Children should learn to express their needs and opinions in a clear and assertive manner, without being aggressive. Assertiveness involves standing up for oneself while respecting others, which is a crucial balance in conflict resolution.

Negotiation Skills: Negotiation is about giving and taking. Children can be taught to negotiate fairly, which might mean taking turns, sharing resources, or working out a plan that allows both parties to get some of what they want.

Strategies for Teaching Conflict Resolution

Incorporating conflict resolution skills into daily life involves intentional strategies that parents and educators can use:

Role-Playing: One effective way to teach conflict resolution is through role-playing various scenarios. This strategy allows children to practice and internalize different ways of handling disputes.

Modeling: Children learn a great deal from observing adults. When parents and teachers handle conflicts calmly and constructively, they provide a powerful model for children to emulate.

Guided Conflict Resolution: When conflicts arise, adults can guide children through the process of resolving the conflict. This involves helping them to articulate their feelings, listen to each other, and brainstorm solutions together.

Setting Clear Rules: Clear rules about acceptable behavior during conflicts can help prevent escalation. These rules might include no name-calling, no physical aggression, and taking turns to speak.

Encouraging Reflection: After a conflict has been resolved, encourage children to reflect on how the situation was handled and what they learned. This reflection can reinforce positive behaviors and provide an opportunity to discuss what could be improved next time.

Creating a Supportive Environment

A supportive environment where children feel safe and valued is crucial for teaching conflict resolution. Such an environment encourages open communication and makes it easier for children to express their feelings and needs without fear of ridicule or punishment.

Conflict resolution skills are vital for children's social and emotional development. By learning to manage conflicts effectively, children gain the ability to navigate complex social situations and build stronger relationships. The skills learned through effective conflict management not only serve children during their school years but also lay the foundation for their future personal and professional relationships. Teaching these skills requires a consistent approach, incorporating practice, modeling, and reinforcement, all of which contribute to children becoming adept at resolving conflicts amicably and effectively.

"Emotions are the colors of the soul; learning to understand and manage them paints a masterpiece of experience that enriches every aspect of life."

&

XIV

The Power of Listening

Listening is a fundamental skill for effective communication and is crucial for developing empathy and understanding in interpersonal relationships. Cultivating active listening skills in children is not only about teaching them to hear words but also to understand the deeper meanings behind them. Active listening involves full engagement and attention to the speaker, fostering a deeper connection and comprehension. By enhancing these skills, children learn to interact more effectively and empathetically with others, paving the way for more meaningful relationships and better conflict resolution.

Understanding Active Listening

Active listening is a multifaceted skill that involves several components:

Attention: Giving full attention to the speaker without distractions.

Acknowledgment: Showing the speaker that their message is being received through nods or verbal affirmations like "I see" or "I understand."

Feedback: Providing feedback that clarifies and confirms understanding of the message.

Empathy: Engaging emotionally with the speaker by understanding their feelings and perspectives.

Patience: Allowing the speaker to express themselves at their own pace without rushing them or interrupting.

These components help children not only hear but also empathize with the speaker, making it a powerful tool for emotional and social learning.

Benefits of Active Listening

Active listening has numerous benefits for children, including:

Improved Peer Relationships: By listening actively, children learn more about their peers' thoughts and feelings, which can lead to stronger, more empathetic relationships.

Enhanced Learning: Active listening in educational settings increases comprehension and retention of information, which can improve academic performance.

Better Conflict Resolution: Understanding all sides of a conversation helps children negotiate solutions more effectively, leading to healthier resolutions of conflicts.

Increased Empathy: Listening actively helps children understand and relate to the emotions of others, which is essential for developing empathy.

Teaching Active Listening Skills

Teaching children to be active listeners can be approached through various strategies:

Modeling Active Listening: Adults should model active listening by giving children their full attention during conversations. This demonstrates respect for the speaker and shows children how to listen effectively.

Listening Games: Games that require listening and following instructions can be fun and effective ways to practice active listening. For example, playing "Simon Says" requires careful listening to details and can be an enjoyable way for children to improve their listening skills.

Role-Playing: Engaging children in role-playing exercises can help them practice listening and responding. Role-playing various scenarios can also help children understand how active listening can improve communications.

Discussion and Debriefing: After a group activity or storytime, have a discussion where children are asked to recall and discuss what they heard. This not only improves listening skills but also comprehension and critical thinking.

Teaching Mindfulness: Encouraging mindfulness practices can enhance children's ability to focus and pay attention. Simple breathing exercises or short periods of meditation can help calm the mind and improve concentration.

Encouraging Feedback

Part of active listening involves learning how to give and receive feedback constructively:

Expressing Thoughts and Feelings: Teach children to express their thoughts and feelings about what they've heard. This can help clarify misunderstandings and deepen their understanding of the conversation.

Asking Questions: Encourage children to ask questions about things they don't understand. This not only promotes better understanding but also engagement in the conversation.

Summarizing and Paraphrasing: Teach children to summarize or paraphrase what they've heard. This practice confirms that they have understood the message correctly and shows the speaker they are truly listening.

Creating an Environment That Fosters Listening

Creating a supportive environment that encourages active listening involves:

Reducing Distractions: Minimize noise and distractions that can interfere with listening. A quieter environment helps children focus better on the conversation.

Establishing Listening as a Value: Make listening an explicit value in the home or classroom. Recognize and praise children when they demonstrate good listening behaviors.

Encouraging Turn-Taking: During discussions, encourage children to take turns speaking and listening. This teaches them the importance of giving everyone a chance to share their thoughts.

Cultivating active listening skills in children is crucial for their social and emotional development. These skills enhance empathy, improve communication, and help children build stronger relationships. By teaching children to listen actively, we equip them with tools essential for success in interpersonal interactions and broaden their understanding of the world around them. Active listening not only enriches the listener's life but also makes the speaker feel valued and understood, fostering a more empathetic and connected community.

"The journey of emotional intelligence is not paved with certainty but with moments of clarity and confusion, each teaching us more about who we are."

XV

Emotional Intelligence and Special Needs

Emotional intelligence (EI) is crucial for all children, including those with special needs. These children may face unique challenges in understanding and managing emotions, making it essential to adapt EI techniques to meet their specific requirements. Enhancing emotional intelligence in children with special needs can lead to improved social interactions, better emotional regulation, and overall greater success in navigating daily challenges.

Understanding the Importance of EI for Children with Special Needs

Children with special needs, including those with autism spectrum disorders, ADHD, sensory processing disorders, and other developmental disabilities, often experience difficulties with social cues, emotional regulation, and communication. These challenges can make it hard for them to form and maintain relationships, manage classroom settings, and cope with changes or stressful situations.

Emotional intelligence skills are particularly valuable for these children as they provide them with tools to better understand their own emotions and those of others, enhance their communication abilities, and develop more effective coping strategies. These skills are not just crucial for personal development but are also vital for academic and social success.

Adapting EI Techniques for Children with Special Needs

Adapting emotional intelligence techniques for children with special needs involves several tailored strategies that consider their specific limitations and strengths:

Simplified Language and Clear Communication: Using simple, clear, and consistent language helps in teaching emotional intelligence concepts to children with special needs. Visual aids such as pictures, emoticons, and video models can also be highly effective in illustrating emotional concepts and expected behaviors.

Structured Learning Environments: Children with special needs often benefit from structured environments where routines are predictable. This predictability can help in managing anxiety and making it easier for them to focus on learning EI skills.

Individualized Learning Approaches: Each child with special needs is unique, and adapting EI education to fit individual learning styles and needs is crucial. This might involve focusing more on non-verbal communication for a child with verbal communication difficulties or incorporating physical activities for a child with hyperactivity.

Using Technology and Assistive Tools: Technology can be a powerful aid in teaching EI. Apps and software designed to teach emotion recognition, emotional regulation, and social skills can be particularly beneficial for children who are visual learners or who engage more effectively with interactive learning tools.

Consistency Across Settings: Applying and reinforcing EI teachings consistently across different settings—home, school, and social environments—helps solidify these skills. Consistency provides the repetitive learning experiences necessary for children with special needs to internalize and apply their emotional intelligence skills.

Social Stories and Role-Playing: Social stories that depict various social situations and appropriate emotional responses can be extremely helpful. Role-playing these scenarios allows children to practice and prepare for real-life interactions.

Emotional Regulation Techniques: Techniques such as deep breathing, sensory activities, or quiet time can be customized to help children with special needs manage overwhelming emotions. These techniques should be tailored to each child's specific sensory preferences and triggers.

Empathy Development Through Concrete Examples: Developing empathy can be challenging for children with special needs. Using concrete examples of feelings and emphasizing the cause-and-effect relationship in social interactions can help make the concept of empathy more accessible.

Feedback and Positive Reinforcement: Positive reinforcement is effective for children with special needs. Immediate and specific feedback about what they are doing right can encourage continued effort and improvement in EI skills.

Professional Guidance and Therapy: Working with professionals who specialize in special education and therapy can provide additional support in developing EI. Therapists can offer specialized strategies and interventions tailored to the child's specific challenges.

Supporting Emotional Growth in Children with Special Needs

Supporting emotional growth in children with special needs requires patience, understanding, and a commitment to finding the most effective ways to teach EI. Parents and educators should collaborate closely to ensure that learning strategies are consistent and tailored to the individual needs of each child.

Adapting emotional intelligence techniques for children with special needs is not only possible but essential. These adaptations can provide these children with the necessary skills to understand and manage their emotions, enhance their interactions with others, and navigate their environments more effectively. With the right strategies and support, children with special needs can achieve significant improvements in their emotional and social functioning, leading to better outcomes in school and later life.

"Building resilience in children is building the future's backbone, strong enough to withstand setbacks and wise enough to cherish every victory."

☙

XVI

Cultural Influences on Emotional Development

Culture plays a pivotal role in shaping emotional development and emotional intelligence. The norms, values, and practices inherent in different cultures influence how emotions are perceived, expressed, and managed. Understanding the impact of cultural contexts on emotional intelligence is crucial for fostering an inclusive, empathetic, and effective approach to education and interpersonal relationships.

The Role of Culture in Emotional Development

Culture defines the ways in which emotions are experienced and communicated. It affects everything from the recognition and expression of emotions to the strategies people use for emotional regulation. Cultural norms dictate which emotions can be openly displayed and which are to be controlled, shaping an individual's emotional experiences from a very young age.

For instance, in some cultures, expressing emotions like anger or sadness publicly is frowned upon, encouraging individuals to develop internal coping mechanisms. In contrast, other cultures may encourage open emotional expression as a way of sharing experiences and strengthening community bonds.

Understanding Emotional Expression Across Cultures

Different cultures have unique emotional vocabularies and expressions. For example, some Asian cultures value the concept of 'saving face' and thus may discourage direct expressions of conflict or negative emotions. Conversely, Mediterranean or Latin American cultures often embrace and encourage vivid expressions of feelings.

Children learn these cultural norms primarily through their family and community, which influence how they express emotions and manage interpersonal interactions. As they grow, their understanding of emotional norms can either facilitate or hinder their interactions, especially in culturally diverse settings.

Cultural Differences in Emotional Regulation

Cultural background also influences emotional regulation strategies. In collectivist cultures, where the group's well-being is prioritized over individual desires, emotional regulation might focus more on maintaining harmony and collective morale. This might involve suppressing personal distress to avoid burdening others. In individualistic cultures, personal authenticity might be emphasized, encouraging individuals to express their emotions more freely as a form of self-expression and authenticity.

Emotional Intelligence and Multicultural Interactions

As societies become more globalized, the ability to understand and adapt to different emotional norms becomes increasingly important. Emotional intelligence in multicultural contexts involves recognizing cultural differences in emotional expression and developing the flexibility to adjust one's behavior in culturally appropriate ways.

For children, learning to navigate these differences can enhance their social and emotional development. It can prepare them for a globalized world where they are more likely to interact with people from diverse backgrounds.

Teaching Emotional Intelligence in Culturally Diverse Settings

Educators and parents can adopt several strategies to teach children about cultural influences on emotional development:

Cultural Awareness Education: Incorporate lessons that explore different cultures' emotional norms and practices. This can help children appreciate cultural diversity and its impact on emotional expressions and relationships.

Inclusive Environment: Create an environment that respects and celebrates cultural differences. This setting should encourage children to share their cultural practices and emotions, fostering a mutual understanding among peers.

Role-Playing and Scenarios: Use role-playing exercises to simulate situations that involve cultural conflicts or misunderstandings. This can help children develop practical skills for empathy and adaptability in real-life interactions.

Discussion and Reflection: Encourage children to discuss how culture affects their own emotions and those of others. Reflective practices can deepen their understanding and enhance their ability to apply this knowledge in social interactions.

Use of Multicultural Literature and Media: Introduce books, films, and other media that represent diverse cultures and emotional contexts. This exposure can broaden children's horizons and enhance their understanding of how different people experience and express emotions.

Supporting Children in Multicultural Emotional Learning

Supporting children as they learn to navigate cultural differences in emotional expression involves ongoing guidance and encouragement. It requires parents and educators to be culturally sensitive and aware of their own biases and assumptions about emotions.

Cultural influences play a significant role in shaping emotional intelligence by dictating norms around emotional expression and regulation. By understanding and respecting these cultural differences, children can develop a more nuanced and comprehensive approach to managing their emotions and interacting with others. Teaching children to recognize and adapt to these cultural nuances is essential in preparing them for successful interactions in a diverse world, enhancing both their personal growth and their ability to contribute positively to society.

"In the face of adversity, emotional intelligence is
the quiet voice that guides us through the storm
with grace and wisdom."

XVII

Resilience: Bouncing Back from Setbacks

Resilience is the ability to recover from difficulties or adapt to challenging situations with flexibility and strength. For children, developing resilience is crucial for navigating the ups and downs of growing up and learning. Fostering resilience in children not only helps them manage current challenges but also prepares them for future obstacles, enhancing their ability to thrive despite adversities.

Understanding Resilience in Children

Resilience in children involves more than just bouncing back from a setback; it includes learning from the experience and emerging stronger than before. This capacity is influenced by a variety of factors, including personality traits, family dynamics, and the broader social environment. Resilient children are often characterized by optimism, good problem-solving skills, and the ability to regulate emotions effectively.

Strategies to Foster Resilience

Several strategies can be employed to help children develop resilience:

Building Strong Relationships: Strong, supportive relationships with parents, caregivers, teachers, and peers are the cornerstone of resilience. Secure attachments make children feel safe to explore their world and face challenges, knowing they have a supportive network to back them up.

Encouraging Positive Thinking: Helping children develop a positive outlook can significantly affect their ability to cope with stress and setbacks. Teach children to see failures as opportunities to learn rather than insurmountable obstacles. This can involve shifting focus from what went wrong to what can be done differently next time.

Developing Problem-Solving Skills: Equip children with the skills to identify problems, think through solutions, and decide on the best course of action. This not only helps them deal with immediate challenges but also instills a sense of competence and control.

Promoting Self-Efficacy: Encourage children to take on tasks they can handle and then gradually increase the challenges as their abilities grow. Success in these tasks builds confidence and a belief in their ability to influence events around them.

Teaching Emotional Regulation: Learning to manage and understand emotions is crucial for resilience. Teach children techniques for coping with negative emotions, such as deep breathing, relaxation exercises, or expressing feelings through words or art.

Creating Opportunities for Personal Achievement: Encourage children to engage in activities that provide a sense of accomplishment. Whether it's sports, arts, or academic achievements, feeling competent and self-assured promotes resilience.

Maintaining Routines: Routines provide a sense of security and predictability that can be comforting during times of stress. While flexibility is important, having a basic structure for daily activities can help children feel more stable and grounded.

Encouraging Physical Activity: Physical health impacts psychological well-being, and regular physical activity is a powerful stress reducer. Activities like team sports not only improve fitness but also offer social support and a chance to develop other resilience skills, such as cooperation and conflict resolution.

Fostering Social Skills: Being able to communicate clearly, listen well, share, negotiate, and empathize with others helps children build and maintain relationships. These skills are essential for resilience, as they allow children to seek help and garner support when needed.

Modeling Resilient Behaviors: Children learn a lot from observing the adults in their lives. By modeling resilience—how to cope with stress, overcome challenges, and recover from setbacks—parents and educators can provide a blueprint for children to follow.

Supporting Children's Resilient Growth

Supporting the development of resilience in children requires a proactive approach that includes providing them with challenges as well as the tools to overcome them. It involves teaching them to think critically about obstacles and failures and to view these experiences as part of the learning process.

Resilience is a critical skill that enables children to navigate the complexities of life with confidence and optimism. By fostering resilience through supportive relationships, teaching problem-solving and emotional regulation skills, and encouraging a positive outlook, parents and educators can prepare children to face life's challenges with courage and grace. These strategies not only help children in the immediate sense but also lay the foundation for their long-term emotional health and well-being, equipping them with the skills they need to thrive throughout their lives.

"Social skills are not just about making friends but about weaving the fabric of community, stitched together with threads of understanding and respect."

XVIII

Celebrating Success and Handling Failure

Teaching children how to navigate both success and failure is crucial for their emotional and personal development. How children learn to handle these experiences can profoundly affect their self-esteem, resilience, and overall mental health. Celebrating successes and managing failures in healthy ways not only prepares children for the ups and downs of life but also instills in them the virtues of humility and perseverance.

The Importance of Celebrating Success

Celebrating successes, big or small, helps reinforce children's efforts and achievements, boosting their confidence and motivation. It teaches them to take pride in their accomplishments and appreciate the hard work that led to those successes. However, it is important that celebrations focus not just on outcomes but also on the effort and progress made, regardless of whether the ultimate goal was achieved.

Strategies for Celebrating Success

Positive Reinforcement: Use positive reinforcement to acknowledge children's successes. This can be through verbal praise, a reward system, or simply spending quality time together. The key is to make the reinforcement specific to their effort or achievement.

Encourage Self-Appreciation: Teach children to appreciate their own efforts independently. Encourage them to reflect on what they did well and how it made them feel. This builds internal motivation and self-satisfaction that does not solely rely on external validation.

Share the Joy: Encourage children to share their successes with others. This not only strengthens social bonds but also allows them to express pride in their achievements, which reinforces positive feelings and confidence.

Handling Failure Constructively

While success is important, teaching children to handle failure is arguably more crucial. Failure is an inevitable part of life and learning to cope with it effectively is essential for developing resilience and perseverance.

Strategies for Handling Failure

Normalize Failure: Teach children that failure is a normal part of learning and growth. Everyone experiences setbacks and mistakes; what matters is how they respond to these challenges.

Focus on Effort and Growth: Help children understand that their value does not diminish because of failure. Encourage them to focus on the effort they put in and what they can learn from the experience to grow stronger or do better in the future.

Problem-Solving: Encourage children to see failure as a problem to be solved rather than a barrier to success. Discuss what didn't work and why, and brainstorm possible solutions or alternative approaches for the future.

Emotional Support: Provide emotional support when children fail. Listen to their concerns and validate their feelings, but also help them regain perspective and encourage them to try again.

Modeling Resilience: Show children how to handle setbacks and failures gracefully by modeling this behavior yourself. Share your own experiences of overcoming failures and what you learned from them.

Balancing Emotions in Success and Failure

Teaching children to balance their emotional responses to both success and failure is vital. They need to learn how to stay humble in success and hopeful in failure.

Teach Emotional Regulation: Provide children with strategies to manage their emotions, whether they're feeling overly elated or deeply disappointed. Techniques like deep breathing, mindfulness, and taking time to reflect can help manage emotional highs and lows.

Set Realistic Expectations: Help children set achievable goals and have realistic expectations about outcomes. This helps mitigate feelings of failure when goals are not met and keeps successes from leading to overconfidence.

Encourage Perspective-Taking: Teach children to see things from different angles. Understanding that success or failure is often not just about individual efforts but also involves external factors can help them maintain a balanced perspective.

Effectively teaching children how to celebrate success and handle failure is crucial for their development into well-rounded, emotionally intelligent individuals. By encouraging positive reinforcement, focusing on effort and growth, normalizing failure, and teaching emotional regulation, parents and educators can equip children with the necessary skills to handle whatever successes or setbacks life may throw at them. These lessons in emotional navigation not only enhance their current academic and social endeavors but also prepare them for future challenges and opportunities in life.

"Every failure encountered in childhood is an invitation to rise, an opportunity to teach resilience that will serve as the cornerstone of future successes."

જી

XIX

Preparing for Adolescence: Transitioning Emotional Intelligence Skills

Adolescence is a critical developmental period marked by significant physical, emotional, and psychological changes. As children transition into their teenage years, the emotional intelligence (EI) skills they have developed during childhood become increasingly important. These skills help them navigate the complexities of adolescence, including shifting social dynamics, greater academic pressures, and evolving self-identity. Preparing children for this transition by reinforcing and adapting EI skills is crucial for their well-being and success during these formative years.

Understanding the Importance of EI in Adolescence

Emotional intelligence during adolescence influences a wide range of outcomes, from academic performance to social relationships and mental health. Teenagers with high EI tend to have better control over their emotions, can communicate more effectively with peers and adults, and are better equipped to handle the stresses and challenges of teenage life. They are also more likely to engage in positive social behaviors and avoid risky behaviors.

Strategies for Transitioning EI Skills into Adolescence

Enhancing Self-Awareness: As children approach adolescence, encourage them to become more aware of their emotions and how these emotions affect their thoughts and behaviors. This can be facilitated through regular discussions about feelings, journaling, or mindfulness practices. These activities help teens recognize their emotional triggers and understand the impact of their emotional responses on their decisions and relationships.

Promoting Self-Management: Adolescents face many situations that require effective emotion regulation, from coping with academic stress to managing peer pressure. Teaching techniques such as deep breathing, meditation, or physical exercise can help teenagers manage their emotions healthily. Encouraging hobbies or interests that allow for emotional expression, such as music, art, or sports, also supports emotional regulation.

Fostering Social Awareness: Social dynamics become more complex in adolescence, with an increased focus on peer relationships and social belonging. Enhancing social awareness skills involves teaching teens to recognize and interpret the social and emotional cues of others accurately. Role-playing, discussing diverse social scenarios, and encouraging empathetic listening can improve their ability to navigate social situations and develop empathy.

Improving Relationship Management: Adolescents need to learn how to maintain and cultivate relationships effectively. This includes understanding how to communicate clearly, resolve conflicts amicably, express needs and boundaries, and show appreciation and support for others. Activities that involve teamwork and cooperative projects can be excellent for practicing these skills.

Encouraging Responsible Decision-Making: As children transition into adolescence, they encounter more opportunities to make independent decisions. Teaching them to consider the emotional and interpersonal consequences of their decisions is vital. Discuss scenarios involving moral dilemmas, peer pressure, and personal goals to enhance their decision-making skills in the context of emotional intelligence.

Modeling Emotional Intelligence: Parents, educators, and other adult role models play a crucial role in modeling emotional intelligence. Demonstrating effective emotional management, empathy, and constructive communication in everyday interactions reinforces these skills for adolescents.

Creating a Supportive Environment: Adolescence is often a time of emotional turbulence. Creating an environment where teens feel safe expressing their emotions and discussing their challenges without judgment is crucial for emotional development. Regular family meetings, one-on-one check-ins, and providing access to mental health resources can all contribute to a supportive emotional climate.

Building Resilience to Setbacks: Adolescence inevitably involves setbacks, whether in academics, relationships, or personal goals. Encouraging a growth mindset—that challenges and failures are opportunities to learn and grow rather than insurmountable obstacles—can help teens build resilience. Celebrating efforts rather than outcomes, and sharing stories of personal and family challenges that were overcome, can reinforce this perspective.

Preparing for Future Challenges

As adolescents develop their emotional intelligence, they also prepare for future challenges in adulthood. The skills acquired during this critical period lay the groundwork for adult relationships, professional success, and personal well-being. Therefore, it is essential to continuously support and reinforce EI development during these years.

Preparing children for adolescence involves a strategic focus on enhancing and adapting their emotional intelligence skills to meet the challenges of the teenage years. By fostering self-awareness, self-management, social awareness, and relationship management skills, parents and educators can help adolescents navigate this complex stage of life effectively. These efforts not only support their current adjustment but also set a foundation for continued growth and success in their adult lives.

"As children grow, their emotional intelligence
lights the way, turning obstacles into opportunities
for growth and self-discovery."

XX

A Lifelong Journey: EI Beyond Childhood

Emotional Intelligence (EI) is not just a developmental goal for childhood but a lifelong journey that continues to enrich personal, social, and professional aspects of life well into adulthood. The skills associated with EI—such as recognizing and managing one's own emotions, understanding others' emotions, and handling interpersonal relationships judiciously and empathetically—are fundamental to achieving personal satisfaction, relationship success, and professional achievements. Understanding the long-term benefits of emotional intelligence can help underscore its importance and encourage continued development throughout one's life.

Foundational Aspects of Emotional Intelligence

Emotional intelligence encompasses several key areas:

Self-awareness – Recognizing one's own emotions and their impact on thoughts and behavior.

Self-regulation – Managing or redirecting one's disruptive emotions and adapting to changing circumstances.

Motivation – Harnessing emotions to pursue goals with energy and persistence.

Empathy – Understanding, recognizing, and considering other people's emotions, an essential part of developing social skills.

Social skills – Managing relationships to move people in desired directions, whether in leading, negotiating, or working as part of a team.

These components of EI do not merely facilitate smoother interactions on a day-to-day basis; they also provide a robust framework for personal growth and fulfillment across the lifespan.

Long-Term Benefits of Emotional Intelligence

Personal Well-being: High EI contributes significantly to personal well-being and mental health. Individuals with strong emotional intelligence are better at managing stress, have higher self-esteem, and are generally more optimistic about life. Their ability to understand and regulate emotions protects them against the adverse effects of stress and mental strain.

Relationship Success: EI is crucial for building and maintaining healthy relationships. The empathy and communication skills that form an integral part of emotional intelligence enable individuals to form deeper connections, resolve conflicts effectively, and understand and meet the emotional needs of others. These skills are vital in personal relationships, contributing to more satisfying and enduring partnerships and friendships.

Professional Effectiveness: In the workplace, EI has been linked to better leadership abilities and higher performance. Leaders with high emotional intelligence can manage their teams more effectively, inspire and motivate their employees, and navigate the complexities of workplace dynamics. Moreover, employees with high EI are often more adaptable and better at handling pressures and demands of their roles.

Social Interaction: Emotional intelligence enhances an individual's capacity to function in social settings. The nuanced understanding of social cues and norms improves interactions and public conduct, making socially intelligent individuals more adept at navigating diverse social landscapes.

Academic Success: For students, EI contributes to better academic performance as it enhances concentration, motivation, and the ability to relate to peers and educators. Emotional intelligence supports a learning environment where students are more engaged and better able to handle the stresses and challenges of academic life.

Cultivating EI Throughout Life

Developing EI is a continuous process, and its cultivation can be intentionally integrated into daily life through several practices:

Continuous Learning: Commit to lifelong learning about emotional intelligence. Reading, workshops, and therapy can all contribute to deeper understanding and better practice.

Mindfulness and Reflection: Engage in mindfulness practices that enhance self-awareness. Regular reflection on one's emotional states and reactions can deepen self-understanding and facilitate better emotional management.

Seek Feedback: Open oneself to feedback about how one's actions affect others. Feedback is a powerful tool for growth in emotional intelligence, particularly in understanding and developing social skills.

Practice Empathy: Make a conscious effort to see things from others' perspectives. This practice not only improves empathy but also enriches interpersonal interactions and relationships.

Build Social Networks: Invest in building and maintaining diverse social networks. Interacting with a wide range of people can provide varied experiences that challenge and refine emotional and social skills.

The journey of developing emotional intelligence is lifelong and dynamic. The skills learned in childhood need to be nurtured and adapted as an individual grows into adulthood and faces new challenges and life changes. The benefits of a high EI are profound and wide-reaching, impacting nearly every aspect of life. By continuing to develop emotional intelligence throughout one's life, an individual not only enhances personal and professional well-being but also contributes positively to the lives of those around them. This ongoing development of EI is essential for a fulfilling and harmonious life.

"Handling emotions with intelligence and care teaches children that while feelings are transient, the lessons learned from managing them last a lifetime."

಄

Citation And References

This book represents the culmination of extensive research and meticulous analysis, incorporating a diverse range of sources, including numerous books, scholarly studies, and personal experiences. Additionally, I have scoured various websites to gather relevant information and data essential for the compilation of this work. I have taken every precaution to ensure the accuracy of the information presented and have diligently cited all sources to acknowledge their contributions.

Despite these efforts, the possibility of inadvertent errors remains. I deeply value the insights of my readers and appreciate any feedback that can help identify and rectify such inaccuracies. I encourage you to bring any discrepancies to my attention.

Your feedback is not only welcome but crucial, as it will aid in correcting current editions and enhancing the content of future ones. I am committed to maintaining the highest standards of accuracy and reliability in my work and thank you for your support and understanding.

Additionally, I firmly uphold the principle of freedom of speech and expression as guaranteed under Article 19(1)(a) of the Constitution of India, and I respect the diverse viewpoints and expressions of all readers.

Other Books Of The Author

1. Empowering Minds: A Journey into Women's Self-Discovery and Power
2. The Dynamics of Motivation: Catalyzing Thought into Action
3. Meditation and Mental Well Being: The Path to Inner Peace and Clarity
4. The Psychology of Child Education: Nurturing Future Generations
5. Ethical Enlightenment: A Modern Guide to Living with Integrity
6. Voices of Empowerment: Stories of Women Rising Against Odds
7. Social Psychology in Everyday Life: Understanding Human Connections
8. The Essence of Motivational Speaking: Inspiring Change in Others
9. Balancing Acts: Women, Work, and the Will to Lead
10. Guiding with Grace: Raising Children with Compassion and Awareness
11. The Power of Positive Aging: Embracing Life After Fifty
12. Building Resilient Communities: Social Work in Action
13. The Ethical Educator: Principles for Teaching and Learning
14. From Insight to Impact: Social Psychology for a Better World
15. The Ethics of Empathy: A Guide to Ethical Living
16. The Science of Empowering the Self: Navigating Life's Challenges with Psychological Wisdom
17. The Mindful Conscious Leader: Meditation Techniques for Modern Management
18. Pioneering Spirit: Women's Pathways to Leadership and Empowerment
19. Feeling to Healing: The Role of Emotional Intelligence in Child Development
20. Transformative Talks and Words of Inspiration: Insights into Motivational Oratory

❧

CONTACT

Dr. Minakshi Bansal
Social Activist
Ahmedabad, Gujarat, Bharat
minakshiindiag20@yahoo.com

|| LOKAHA SAMASTHAHA SUKHINO BHAVANTU ||

www.ingramcontent.com/pod-product-compliance
Lightning Source LLC
Chambersburg PA
CBHW020838120726
48008CB00001B/11